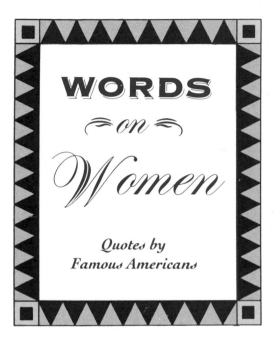

WORDS

⟨ on ⟩

Women

Quotes by
Famous Americans

Edited by
Evelyn L. Beilenson and Sharon Melnick

With Illustrations by
Martha Holland Bartsch

PETER PAUPER PRESS, INC.
WHITE PLAINS · NEW YORK

Table of Contents

Introduction

The only question left to be settled now is: Are women persons?
                                    Susan B. Anthony

Throughout the centuries, men and women have struggled to answer Susan B. Anthony's simple yet pithy question. In the most literal sense, women are, of course, persons. But are women really "persons" in the way that (male) society views them? Do they have the rights and have they received the recognition accorded fully functioning human beings? The quotes in this book suggest that the matter has not been resolved in all its aspects for many American men and women.

Issues which concerned Abigail Adams and Benjamin Franklin are issues still relevant to Betty Ford and Dustin Hoffman. Compare Louisa May Alcott's view that "women have been called queens for a long time—but the kingdom given them isn't worth ruling" with Elizabeth Janeway's point that women wouldn't still be called "baby" if they had in fact really "come a long way."

While considerable progress has clearly been made on a political and social level, we are only beginning to see changes in men's statements that may presage their genuine acceptance of women as equals. In contrast, the women's quotations reflect a strongly developed acceptance of themselves which we can trace from women's nineteenth century struggles for rights as persons to their modern-day celebration of womanhood.

Prior to the advent of the feminist revolution of the last twenty years, the recorded statements of most prominent American men evidenced disdain for or at least an undervaluing of women. The editors, in order to present a more balanced view of women, chose in many cases the words of men who show they like women. Nonetheless, most men appear to find women difficult to understand, and therefore untouchable, mysterious, fragile and in some ways incomplete. Thus, even when men put women on a pedestal (or in Woody Allen's case, "under a pedestal"), they seem to reveal an underlying feeling of superiority.

It is important to note that men discuss women in relation to themselves whereas women quoted in this book are more concerned with their persons and their rights. Women, in analyzing themselves relative to men, express bitterness about their treatment as second-class citizens and show a determination to overcome their subjugation. Modern-day women even have the temerity to speak of men as inferior to themselves! In reading *Words on Women*, we register the sense of pride felt by women in all different fields and appreciate their words of encouragement to the next generation.

Perhaps, given human nature, the path to personhood and equality lies in the equitable sharing of power, both public and private, with men. As Katharine Graham suggests:

> *The thing women must do to rise to power is redefine their femininity. Once, power was considered a masculine attribute. In fact, power has no sex.*

We invite you to savor the quotations in *Words on Women*—to laugh a little, think a little, and reflect on the future of the women of America.

E.L.B.   S.M.

Entertainers and Athletes

Anyone who says he can see through women is missing a lot.

GROUCHO MARX

The trouble with some women is that they get all excited about nothing—and then marry him.

CHER

Women are not forgiven for aging. Bob Redford's lines of distinction are my old-age wrinkles.

JANE FONDA

I tended to place my wife under a pedestal.

WOODY ALLEN

MATRON: "I am sure that a man of your wide experience favors clubs for women." W.C. FIELDS: "Indubitably, madam, indubitably. But only if every other form of persuasion fails."

If you want a thing well done, get a couple of old broads to do it.

BETTE DAVIS

The American woman's ambitions are too high. In Europe a woman decides early what type she will be—mother, cook or siren. Women here want to be all of these and also run Wall Street.

ALISTAIR COOKE

I'm tough, ambitious, and I know exactly what I want. If that makes me a bitch, okay.

MADONNA

I was exploring the ways women and men related to me as Dorothy and I'd never been related to that way before in my life— having men meet me, say hello and immediately start looking over my shoulder trying to find an attractive woman! . . . I would get very hostile: I wanted to get even with them.

DUSTIN HOFFMAN

I don't mind living in a man's world as long as I can be a woman in it.

MARILYN MONROE

After my screen test, the director clapped his hands gleefully and yelled: "She can't talk! She can't act! She's sensational!"

AVA GARDNER

I never realized until lately that women were supposed to be the inferior sex.

KATHARINE HEPBURN

A man has to be Joe McCarthy to be called ruthless. All a woman has to do is put you on hold.

MARLO THOMAS

It's a misconception that I'm not in favor of women's lib. I'm very much in favor, and have been trying to get them to take off their bras for years.

BURT REYNOLDS

I never expected to see the days when girls get sunburned in the places they do now.

WILL ROGERS

Women can be pretty in many ways . . . their looks change as you get to know them because you start seeing them from the inside. Their beauty grows on you depending on their personality and their character.

REGGIE JACKSON

12

A woman, I always say, should be like a
good suspense movie: the more left to the
imagination, the more excitement there is.

ALFRED HITCHCOCK

Who says women have to give up femininity
to get equal legal rights? Anyway I don't
want to go through a doorway ahead of a
man—it's more fun to squeeze through
together.

PERLE MESTA

I like a woman with a head on her
shoulders. I hate necks.

STEVE MARTIN

A mature woman doesn't have to push, and
she doesn't have to depend on gimmicks or
beauty aids. It's her attitude toward life that
makes her mature and attractive.

PAUL NEWMAN

13

All women are natural born espionage agents.

EDDIE CANTOR

There are three things a woman can make out of almost anything—a salad, a hat and a quarrel.

JOHN BARRYMORE

Some of the best boy scouts are girls.

GROUCHO MARX

I have an intense desire to return to the womb. Anybody's.

WOODY ALLEN

The reason good women like me and flock to my pictures is that there is a little bit of vampire instinct in every woman.

THEDA BARA

I always tell young men there are three rules: They hate us, we hate them; they're stronger, they're smarter; and most important: they don't play fair.

JACK NICHOLSON

Girls have an unfair advantage over men: if they can't get what they want by being smart, they can get it by being dumb.

YUL BRYNNER

Women are a lot like umpires. They make quick decisions, never reverse them, and they don't think you're safe when you're out.

PETE ROSE

If I have to, I can do anything. I am strong, I am invincible, I am woman.

HELEN REDDY

Writers

After all these years, I see that I was mistaken about Eve in the beginning; it is better to live outside the Garden with her than inside it without her.

MARK TWAIN

If it was woman who put man out of Paradise, it is still woman, and woman only, who can lead him back.

ELBERT HUBBARD

Women are being considered as candidates for Vice President of the United States because it is the worst job in America. It's amazing that men will take it. A job with real power is First Lady. I'd be willing to run for that. As far as the men who are running for President are concerned, they aren't people I would date.

NORA EPHRON

A beautiful woman is a picture which drives all beholders nobly mad.

RALPH WALDO EMERSON

Woman would be more charming if one could fall into her arms without falling into her hands.

AMBROSE BIERCE

Women have been called queens for a long time—but the kingdom given them isn't worth ruling.

LOUISA MAY ALCOTT

If women want any rights they had better take them, and say nothing about it.

HARRIET BEECHER STOWE

Man has his will—but woman has her way!

OLIVER WENDELL HOLMES

18

In the East, women religiously conceal that
they have faces; in the West, that they have
legs. In both cases they make it evident that
they have but little brains.

HENRY DAVID THOREAU

The world has been busy for some centuries
in shutting and locking every door through
which a woman could step into wealth,
except the door of marriage.

HARRIET BEECHER STOWE

Men define intelligence, men define
usefulness, men tell us what is beautiful,
men even tell us what is womanly.

SALLY KEMPTON

One frequently only finds out how really
beautiful a really beautiful woman is after
considerable acquaintance with her; and the
rule applies to Niagara Falls, to majestic
mountains, and to mosques—especially to
mosques.

MARK TWAIN

19

Women have changed in their relationship
to men, but men stand pat just where Adam
did when it comes to dealing with women.
DOROTHY DIX

If I were asked . . . to what the singular
prosperity and growing strength of that
people ought mainly to be attributed, I
should reply: To the superiority of their
women.
ALEXIS DE TOCQUEVILLE

Be not ashamed, woman—your privilege
encloses the rest, and is the exit of the rest;
You are the gates of the body, and you are
the gates of the soul.
WALT WHITMAN
I Sing the Body Electric

A poet looks at the world as a man looks at
a woman.
WALLACE STEVENS

Throughout all of history, books were written with sperm, not menstrual blood.

ERICA JONG

You don't know anything about a woman until you meet her in court.

NORMAN MAILER

Women complain about sex more often than men. Their gripes fall into two major categories: (1) Not enough. (2) Too much.

ANN LANDERS

He's a real wolf: he can take one look at a girl and tell what kind of a past she's going to have.

GEORGE S. KAUFMAN

She had two complexions, A.M. and P.M.

RING LARDNER

There is in every true woman's heart a spark of heavenly fire, which lies dormant in the broad daylight of prosperity, but which kindles up and beams and blazes in the dark hour of adversity.

WASHINGTON IRVING

A good woman inspires a man; a brilliant woman interests him; a beautiful woman fascinates him; and a sympathetic woman gets him.

HELEN ROWLAND

Men have a much better time of it than women; for one thing they marry later; for another thing they die earlier.

H. L. MENCKEN

"Widow" is a harsh and hurtful word. It comes from the Sanskrit and it means "empty." I have been empty too long.

LYNN CAINE

A woman springs a sudden reproach upon
you which provokes a hot retort—and then
she will presently ask you to apologize.

MARK TWAIN

You can lead a horticulture, but you can't
make her think.

DOROTHY PARKER

The most beautiful description of a woman
is by understatement.

WILLIAM FAULKNER

Women are the real architects of society.

HARRIET BEECHER STOWE

Love is the delusion that one woman differs
from another.

H. L. MENCKEN

23

There is nothing like the ticker tape except a woman—nothing that promises, hour after hour, day after day, such sudden developments; nothing that disappoints so often or occasionally fulfills with such unbelievable, passionate magnificence.

WALTER K. GUTMAN

Man forgives woman anything save the wit to outwit him.

MINNA ANTRIM

A woman's strength is the unresistible might of weakness.

RALPH WALDO EMERSON

Women sit, or move to and fro—some old, some young; The young are beautiful—but the old are more beautiful than the young.

WALT WHITMAN

Beautiful Women

There is only one good substitute for the endearments of a sister, and that is the endearments of some other fellow's sister.

JOSH BILLINGS

Men seldom make passes at girls who wear glasses.

DOROTHY PARKER

Ashes to ashes, Dust to dust, If whiskey don't get you, Women must.

UNKNOWN

From Langston Hughes, The Book of Negro Humor.

Woman: the peg on which the wit hangs his jest, the preacher his text, the cynic his grouch and the sinner his justification.

HELEN ROWLAND

Educating a woman is like pouring honey over a fine Swiss watch. It stops working.

KURT VONNEGUT, JR.

25

I think you have to be honest. A lot of women have low libidos. I would say that is true for the majority of married women.

MARABEL MORGAN

We haven't come a long way, we've come a short way. If we hadn't come a short way, no one would be calling us "baby."

ELIZABETH JANEWAY

The fact of the matter is that the prime responsibility of a woman probably is to be on earth long enough to find the best mate possible for herself, and conceive children who will improve the species.

NORMAN MAILER

What is most beautiful in virile men is something feminine; what is most beautiful in feminine women is something masculine.

SUSAN SONTAG

Women speak because they wish to speak, whereas a man speaks only when driven to speech by something outside himself—like, for instance, he can't find any clean socks.

JEAN KERR

Superwoman gets up in the morning and wakes her 2.6 children, feeds them a grade-A breakfast, and . . . then goes upstairs and gets dressed in her Anne Klein suit, and goes off to her $25,000-a-year job doing work which is creative and socially useful. Then she comes home after work and spends a real meaningful hour with her children, because after all it's not the quantity of time, it's the quality of time. Following that, she goes into the kitchen and creates a Julia Child 60-minute gourmet recipe, having a wonderful family dinner discussing the checks and balances of the United States government system. The children go upstairs to bed and she and her husband spend another hour in their own meaningful relationship. They go upstairs and she is multiorgasmic until midnight.

ELLEN GOODMAN

Social Reformers

Pray to God. She will help you.
ALVA VANDERBILT BELMONT

From press, and pulpit, and platform, she
was taught that "to be unknown was her
highest praise," that "dependence was her
best protection," and "her weakness her
sweetest charm."
EMILY COLLINS

That . . . man . . . says women can't have as
much rights as man, cause Christ wasn't a
woman. Where did your Christ come from?
. . . From God and a woman. Man had
nothing to do with him.
SOJOURNER TRUTH

In order that she may be able to give her
hand with dignity, she must be able to stand
alone.

MARGARET FULLER

Our fathers waged a bloody conflict with
England, because *they* were taxed without
being represented . . . *They* were not willing
to be governed by laws which *they* had no
voice in making: but this is the way in
which women are governed in this Republic.

ANGELINA GRIMKÉ

Wherever there is a human being, I see
God-given rights inherent in that being,
whatever may be the sex or complexion.

WILLIAM LLOYD GARRISON

Women have just as much right to an
uninterrupted career as men, and fathers
have just as much responsibility as mothers
for caring for their children or deciding who
will care for them.

DR. BENJAMIN SPOCK

The costume of women should be suited to her wants and necessities. It should conduce at once to her health, comfort, and usefulness; and, while it should not fail also to conduce to her personal adornment, it should make that end of secondary importance.

AMELIA JENKS BLOOMER

I thought that the chief thing to be done in order to equal boys was to be learned and courageous. So I decided to study Greek and learn to manage a horse.

ELIZABETH CADY STANTON

Abraham Lincoln immortalized himself by the emancipation of four million Southern slaves. Speaking for my suffrage coadjutors, we now desire that you, Mr. President, who are already celebrated for so many noble deeds and honourable utterances, immortalize yourself by bringing about the complete emancipation of thirty-six million women.

ELIZABETH CADY STANTON

. . . woman has a thousand ways to attach herself to the governing power of the land and already exerts an honorable influence on the course of legislation. She is the victim of abuses, to be sure, but it cannot be pretended that I think that her cause [is] as urgent as that of ours.

FREDERICK DOUGLASS

The NOW campaign will remind the nation that women's rights were excluded from it [the Constitution] and to this day equality before the law is not guaranteed for women. It should be in the Constitution. It should have been a birth right.

ELEANOR SMEAL

By law, public sentiment, and religion from the time of Moses down to the present day, woman has never been thought of other than a piece of property, to be disposed of at the will and pleasure of man.

SUSAN B. ANTHONY

A successful woman preacher was once asked, "What special obstacles have you met as a woman in the ministry?" "Not one," she answered, "except the lack of a minister's wife."

ANNA GARLIN SPENCER

The institution of marriage makes a parasite of woman, an absolute dependent. It incapacitates her for life's struggle, annihilates her social consciousness, paralyzes her imagination, and then imposes its gracious protection, which is in reality a snare, a travesty on human character.

EMMA GOLDMAN

Engels, on the nineteenth-century family system, said, "Man is the capitalist; woman is the means of production, the factory; children are labor." Today's system of marriage is again "just a way to get cheap labor—economics is all it is."

GLORIA STEINEM

. . . not one man, in the million, . . . no, not in the hundred million, can rise above the belief that Woman was made for *Man*, . . .

MARGARET FULLER

For I am my mother's daughter, and the drums of Africa still beat in my heart. They will not let me rest while there is a single Negro boy or girl without a chance to prove his worth.

MARY MCLEOD BETHUNE

No matter what your fight, don't be ladylike! God almighty made women and the Rockefeller gang of thieves made the ladies.

"MOTHER" MARY JONES

The wrongs of woman have too long slumbered. They now begin to cry for redress. Let them, then, not *ask* as *favor*, but *demand* as *right*, that every civil obstacle be removed out of the way.

LUCRETIA MOTT

If men could become pregnant, abortion would be a sacrament.

FLO KENNEDY

They [women] are confined to conditions of economic dependence based on the sale of their sexuality in marriage, or a variety of prostitutions. Work on a basis of economic independence allows them only a subsistence level of life—often not even that.

KATE MILLETT

The glorification of the "woman's role," then, seems to be in proportion to society's reluctance to treat women as complete human beings; for the less real function that role has, the more it is decorated with meaningless details to conceal its emptiness.

BETTY FRIEDAN

I was a woman before I was an abolitionist. I must speak for the women.

LUCY STONE

Entrepreneurs

I love Mickey Mouse more than any woman
I've ever known.

WALT DISNEY

I am a woman, I am a mother . . . I want to
remain a woman but I want a man's life.

DIANE VON FURSTENBERG

I was taught to think you can always do
anything you want to do if you work hard
enough.

MARY WELLS LAWRENCE

I've always been independent, and I don't
see how it conflicts with femininity.

SYLVIA PORTER

Henry VII . . . He didn't get divorced, he just had their heads chopped off when he got tired of them. That's a good way to get rid of a woman—no alimony.

TED TURNER

The thing women must do to rise to power is redefine their femininity. Once, power was considered a masculine attribute. In fact, power has no sex.

KATHARINE GRAHAM

The skilled woman can invent beauty over and over again with extraordinary effect. The art of inventing beauty transcends class, intellect, age, profession, geography— virtually every cultural and economic barrier.

ESTÉE LAUDER

I've always believed that one woman's success can only help another woman's success.

GLORIA VANDERBILT

If you're making a quarter of a million dollars a year, you think twice about suing your employer [on the ground of sex discrimination].

MURIEL SIEBERT

If you want more legal tender, hire more of the female gender.

BERNICE FITZ-GIBBON

Young women must become more aware and more active. They care about the progress the women's movement has made but they take it for granted.

MURIEL SIEBERT

So many women just don't know how great they really are. They come to us all vogue outside and vague on the inside. It's so rewarding to watch them develop and grow.

MARY KAY ASH

39

Public Figures

Women's place is in the House and in the Senate.

GLORIA SCHAFFER

Even in the freest countries our property is subject to the control and disposal of our partners, to whom the laws have given a sovereign authority.

ABIGAIL ADAMS

Every year we go a step further. Myself, personally, I will not be satisfied until women have a place in the Constitution. President Ford and I have five granddaughters and I feel very strongly about working for their opportunities.

BETTY FORD

It would need more than the 19th Amendment to convince me that there are no differences between men and women, or that legislation cannot take those differences into account.

OLIVER WENDELL HOLMES, JR.

A woman (the same may be said of the other sex) all beautiful and accomplished will, while her hand and heart are undisposed of, turn the heads and set the circle in which she moves on fire. Let her marry, and what is the consequence? The madness *ceases* and all is quiet again. Why? Not because there is any diminution in the charms of the lady, but because there is an end of hope.

GEORGE WASHINGTON

In your amours you should prefer old women to young ones. This you call a paradox, and demand my reasons. They are . . . 8th and lastly: they are so grateful.

BEN FRANKLIN

The manners of women are the surest
criterion by which to determine whether a
republican government is practicable in a
nation or not.

JOHN ADAMS

I consider a [slave] woman who brings a
child every two years as more profitable
than the best man of the farm.

THOMAS JEFFERSON

The tender breasts of ladies were not
formed for political convulsion.

THOMAS JEFFERSON

You can't have a Congress that responds to
the needs of the workingman when there
are practically no people here who represent
him. And you're not going to have a society
that understands its humanity if you don't
have more women in government.

BELLA ABZUG

Women share with men the need for
personal success, even the taste for power,
and no longer are we willing to satisfy those
needs through the achievements of
surrogates, whether husbands, children or
merely role models.

ELIZABETH DOLE

Out of the 93 persons who have sat on the
Supreme Court, not one yet has been a
woman. Too bad, for they always have the
last word, except here, where the last word
really counts.

TOM CLARK

A woman is the only thing I am afraid of
that I know will not hurt me.

ABRAHAM LINCOLN

Are women books? says Hodge, then would
mine were An Almanac, to change her
every year.

BENJAMIN FRANKLIN

44

What is sad for women of my generation is
that they weren't supposed to work if they
had families. What were they to do when
the children were grown—watch the
raindrops coming down the windowpane?

JACQUELINE KENNEDY ONASSIS

The capacity of the female mind for studies
of the highest order cannot be doubted,
having been sufficiently illustrated by
its works of genius, of erudition, and of
science . . .

JAMES MADISON

A woman is like a tea bag; you don't know
her strength until she is in hot water.

NANCY REAGAN

The appointment of a woman to office is an
innovation for which the public is not
prepared, nor am I.

THOMAS JEFFERSON

Sensible and intelligent women do not want to vote. The relative positions to be assumed by man and woman in the working out of our civilization were assigned long ago by a higher intelligence than ours.

GROVER CLEVELAND

[N]o lady dances after marriage. This is founded in solid physical reasons, gestation and nursing leaving little time to a married lady when this exercise can be either safe or innocent.

THOMAS JEFFERSON

Remember, Ginger Rogers did everything Fred Astaire did, but she did it backwards and in high heels.

FAITH WHITTLESEY

Did you ever hear of a great and good man who had not a good mother?

JOHN ADAMS

I never war against females and it is only
the base and cowardly that do . . .

ANDREW JACKSON

We have but one police force, the American
woman.

HERBERT HOOVER

Women have been in everything else—why
not in politics? There's no reason why a
woman shouldn't be in the White House as
President, if she wants to be. But she'll be
sorry when she gets there.

HARRY TRUMAN

I know the influence of womanhood will
guard the home, which is the citadel of
the nation . . . I welcome it as a great
instrument of mercy and a mighty agency
of peace. I want every woman to vote.

CALVIN COOLIDGE

If I were to give advice to older women interested in politics, I'd say yes, go ahead. Get involved! It takes confidence, of course, and I was very fortunate to have instant name recognition and family support, but the main thing is flexibility. I think in some ways women are very flexible and resilient because over the years they've had to be!

NANCY KASSEBAUM

Men and women feel the same inclinations to each other *now* that they always have done, and which they will continue to do until there is a new order of things . . . the passions of your sex are easier raised than allayed.

GEORGE WASHINGTON

The mother is the one supreme asset of national life; she is more important by far than the successful statesman, or businessman, or artist, or scientist.

THEODORE ROOSEVELT

We shall need [women's] moral sense to preserve what is right and fine and worthy in our system of life, as well as to discover just what it is that ought to be purified and reformed. Without their counselings, we shall be only half wise.

WOODROW WILSON

When Harvard men say they have graduated from Radcliffe, then we've made it.

JACQUELINE KENNEDY ONASSIS

When an Italian talks with an American he's inclined to feel a twinge of inferiority. America is rich and strong. Italy is poor. But when he talks to me, he's more at ease. I still represent a big, strong nation but I am a women and he's a man.

CLARE BOOTHE LUCE

Women can always withhold sex from their husbands [to get what they want].

ADMIRAL HYMAN RICKOVER

I want to make a policy statement. I am
unabashedly in favor of women.
LYNDON B. JOHNSON

In passing, also, I would like to say that the
first time Adam had a chance he laid the
blame on women.
LADY NANCY ASTOR

I will feel equality has arrived when we
can elect to office women who are as
incompetent as some of the men who
are already there.
MAUREEN REAGAN

Few decisions are more personal and
intimate, more properly private, or more
basic to individual dignity and autonomy,
than a woman's decision . . . whether to end
her pregnancy.
JUSTICE HARRY BLACKMUN

We women do talk too much, but even then we don't tell half we know.

LADY NANCY ASTOR

So you're the little woman who wrote the book that made this great war.

ABRAHAM LINCOLN
On meeting Harriet Beecher Stowe

History will judge that the decision to pick the first woman to run on the national ticket of either party was a bold and proper step that strengthened our nation.

WALTER MONDALE

As commissioner, I will attempt to see no man is judged by the irrational criteria of race, religion, or national origin. And I assure you I use the word 'man' in the generic sense, for I mean to see that the principle of nondiscrimination becomes a reality for women as well.

ELEANOR HOLMES NORTON

Visionaries and Artists

The recognition by men that women are co-custodians of this planet, although absurdly belated, is one of the most hopeful developments in recent history.

CARL SAGAN

I kissed my first woman and smoked my first cigarette on the same day. I have never had time for tobacco since.

ARTURO TOSCANINI

I have been told that there is no precedent for admitting a woman to practice in the Supreme Court of the United States. The glory of each generation is to make its own precedents. As there was none for Eve in the Garden of Eden, so there need be none for her daughters on entering the colleges, the church, or the courts.

BELVA LOCKWOOD

Women want mediocre men, and men are
working hard to be as mediocre as possible.

MARGARET MEAD

They [girls] were not simply eager to fail
and have done with it, they seemed to be in
a state of anxious conflict over what would
happen if they succeeded. It was almost as
though this conflict was inhibiting their
capacity for achievement.

MATINA HORNER

Woman, having received from her Creator
the same intellectual contribution as man,
has the same right as man to intellectual
culture and development.

MATTHEW VASSAR

There is a growing strength in women—but
it's in the forehead, not in the forearm.

BEVERLY SILLS

54

Being a woman is important for me. But being an artist is more important.

BEVERLY PEPPER

I find that women can be creative in total isolation. I know excellent women artists who do original work without any response to speak of. Maybe they are used to a lack of feedback.

ELAINE DE KOONING

If American women would increase their voting turnout by ten percent, I think we would see an end to all of the budget cuts in programs benefiting women and children.

CORETTA SCOTT KING

No woman can call herself free who does not own or control her body. No woman can call herself free until she can choose consciously whether she will or will not be a mother.

MARGARET SANGER

Women through all ages could have had
physical strength and mental creativity and
still have been feminine. The fact that these
things have been suppressed is the fault of
society.

LOUISE NEVELSON

The evidence indicates that woman is, on
the whole, biologically superior to man.

ASHLEY MONTAGU

The natural superiority of women is a
biological fact, and a socially acknowledged
reality.

ASHLEY MONTAGU

I think what I would ideally like to see in
our society is that sex become an ascribed
rather than an achieved status. That one is
simply born a girl or a boy and that's it.
And no worry about an activity's
defeminizing or emasculating one.

DAVID REISMAN

Appendix

57

61

62